VANUATU

TRAVEL GUIDE

2024

"Island Serenity: A Traveler's Dream Destination"

KYLE WATSON

___Table of Content___

INTRODUCTION

Overview

Welcome to the beautiful archipelago of Vanuatu, where golden beaches meet blue seas and verdant vistas invite visitors to experience a paradise unlike any other. Discover the subtleties of this tropical paradise and why it's a traveler's ideal destination by taking an immersive trip with our comprehensive Vanuatu Travel Guide for 2024.

Welcome to Vanuatu

A feeling of peace envelops you as soon as you set foot on Vanuatu's sandy sands, laying the groundwork for an incredible journey. This introduction provides an overview of the rich cultural tapestry, varied landscapes, and kind hospitality that greets each tourist, acting as your doorway to the heart of the archipelago. Discover the distinctive fusion of customs that makes Vanuatu stand out as a travel destination that combines contemporary appeal with authenticity.

An Overview of This Travel Guide

Get acquainted with the format and goals of this book before exploring the depths of Vanuatu's treasures. Learn how each segment has been carefully designed to address various facets of your trip by providing helpful advice, suggestions, and insider knowledge. This book is meant to be your travel companion for the duration of your adventure, whether you're an experienced tourist looking for off-the-beaten-path adventures or a first-time visitor ready to take in Vanuatu's natural beauty.

Getting Around Vanuatu

Vanuatu's appeal is not limited to its stunning scenery; it also rests on the smooth experience it provides visitors. This guide will provide you with vital information about island navigation, local traditions, and how to make the most of your Vanuatu experience. Get the information that will make your trip more enjoyable overall, from transportation tips to cultural quirks.

Getting There

We'll walk you through the several routes and modes of transportation to start your trip to Vanuatu. Find out when is the best to visit, the international gateways, and travel connections. Learn about the necessary visa and entrance formalities to ensure a seamless arrival while getting ready to take in Vanuatu's breathtaking scenery.

Island Essentials

It's important to comprehend Vanuatu's fundamentals to properly enjoy its marvels. Engage in conversations on the temperature and weather of the archipelago, providing advice on when to visit depending on your interests. Find the linguistic and cultural mosaic that gives your travels a colorful touch. Additionally, this guide offers helpful advice on banking, communication, and money to help you travel throughout Vanuatu with confidence.

Exploring Regions

Vanuatu is a group of varied locations that each provide a distinctive combination of experiences and attractions, rather than simply one single location. Take a virtual tour to discover the hidden gems around the archipelago, from the East Coast's rich cultural heritage to the North Shore's immaculate beaches. Experience the hiking trails of the Central Highlands or unwind in the tranquil South Islands; the options are as diverse as the scenery.

Accommodations

One of the most important factors influencing your Vanuatu experience is where you sleep. This guide presents you with a range of lodging choices to suit varying tastes and price ranges. Vanuatu offers accommodations for every kind of traveler, including boutique hotels with an air of elegance, luxury resorts with jaw-dropping vistas, and affordable stays without sacrificing comfort. Discover distinctive lodging options that guarantee to be more than simply a place to stay but an experience in and of itself.

Culinary Delights

The food scene in Vanuatu is a mouthwatering voyage for the senses. Explore the best of the archipelago's culinary offerings, which range from hotspots that promise a blend of international influences to traditional Vanuatuan specialties that highlight regional tastes. This guide reveals hidden jewels for street food adventuresters who want to experience real flavors while fully soaking up the local atmosphere.

Activities and Excursions

In Vanuatu, there is an experience waiting for you every minute. Indulge in water sports along the coast, immerse yourself in cultural events and festivals, explore the abundant wildlife, or go on day excursions and island hopping. Dive into the multitude of activities that await. Your activity schedule for Vanuatu is provided in this chapter, so you may make the most of every day of discovery and adventure.

Wellness and Relaxation

Beyond its bustling activities, Vanuatu calls people in search of rest and renewal. Explore the health options on the island, which include yoga and meditation institutes for reestablishing your connection to nature and yourself, as well as spa getaways that will soothe your senses. Take comfort in unwinding on the beach, where the soothing sound of the waves serves as your background music.

Practical Travel Tips

Practicality becomes crucial as you explore Vanuatu's paradise. This section encourages responsible tourism, offers helpful advice on health and safety, and packs necessary items. Equip yourself with the information necessary to guarantee a smooth and considerate tour of this magnificent location.

Conclusion

With appreciation for the experiences made and the beauty encountered, bid Vanuatu goodbye. This last section closes with a request for you to consider your voyage, a call for you to share your stories, and an invitation to return to this tropical paradise for more adventures.

Allow the spirit of Vanuatu to capture your senses as you set off on this expedition through the pages of this guide leaving you with treasured memories that last long after your trip is over.

GETTING THERE

Arriving in Vanuatu

Excitement permeates the air as you drop through the turquoise sky to the jewel-toned archipelago of Vanuatu. The magic of this tropical paradise starts the minute your boots hit the ground. From the international airports to the local transit systems that quickly get you to the center of these islands, this chapter is your roadmap for the first stages of your Vanuatu experience.

International Gateways

Through well-connected international ports, Vanuatu welcomes visitors, guaranteeing a seamless journey from your home country to the sun-drenched coasts of the archipelago. Discover the main airports that act as entrance points; each has its appeal and easy access to various parts of Vanuatu. Whether you choose to arrive in the bustling capital city or a more remote location, each gateway sets the tone for the variety of experiences that lie ahead.

Flight Connections

Your route to Vanuatu will be significantly shaped by your connections. Discover the most popular flight paths and airlines that make it easy to go to this tropical paradise. This area offers information to help you choose the flight path that best suits your travel choices, from direct flights to connecting routes that let you visit other places en route.

Local Transportation Options

Once you're there, choose from a variety of transportation choices to best fit your requirements and explore Vanuetu's islands. Engage in conversations about effective public transportation in the area, such as buses, taxis, and rental cars, to make sure you can get to your lodgings with ease. Experience the allure of island hopping coupled with the ease of well-kept infrastructure and roads that make traveling to Vanuatu a pleasure.

Visa and Entry Requirements

To guarantee a smooth arrival, acquaint yourself with the visa and entrance procedures before entering Vanuetuan territory. This section provides you with the information you need to handle the arrival process smoothly by outlining the necessary paperwork, kinds of visas, and entrance requirements. Comprehending the admission procedures is essential to guarantee a pleasant start to your travel, regardless of the length of your stay.

Let your excitement grow as you set out on the journey to arrive in Vanuatu, for there is a world of tropical treasures just waiting to be explored outside the airport gates. Arriving in Vanuatu is more than simply a practical step—it's the start of an adventure that will fully immerse you in the natural beauty, rich culture, and tranquility of this traveler's ideal location.

Transportation Options

Vanuatu has a range of transportation choices to suit various tastes and travel methods, thanks to its dispersed islands and varied sceneries. One of the most important parts of your trip will be learning about this tropical paradise, and this chapter will show you several ways to get around so you may easily tour the archipelago at your speed.

Island Hopping and Boat Services

Indulge in the well-liked activity of island hopping to embrace the island vibe. Explore the network of boat services that link the islands of Vanuatu, offering a useful mode of transit as well as a chance to take in the breathtaking coastline scenery. Island hopping transforms into a picturesque excursion, unveiling undiscovered coves and immaculate beaches all along the route, whether you want to use scheduled boat services or private charters.

Public Transportation

Vanuatu has a well-functioning public transport network that includes buses and small vans that go around the islands. Examine in-depth information about public transportation's timetables, routes, and convenience as a cheap and engaging way to see the archipelago. Public transportation offers a universe of experiences, enabling you to engage with people and take in the everyday rhythm of Vanuatu life, whether you're traveling to major metropolitan areas or isolated villages.

Taxis and Ride-Sharing Services

Taxis and ride-sharing services are easily accessible for those looking for convenience and customized travel experiences. Discover the versatility of private transportation, whether you're heading to a remote beach for a day excursion or just need a speedy ride from the airport to your lodging. Learn how to bargain for a better deal and guarantee a smooth travel while exploring the islands in the luxury and seclusion of your car.

Rental Services: Cars, Bikes, and Scooters

Give yourself the flexibility to freely explore Vanuatu by giving rental services some thought. Regardless of your preference for the freedom of a vehicle for lengthy drives or the spirit of adventure of a scooter for exploring the coast, this section offers information on rental alternatives that are accessible across the islands. Experience the delight of traveling at your speed via winding roads and picturesque landscapes while designing a customized itinerary based on your interests.

Air Travel Between Island Groups

Traveling by plane between the islands is a quick and beautiful way for people who want to make the most of their time and enjoy the amazing aerial views of Vanuatu. Learn more about the regional flights that will quickly and elegantly transport you to various locations around the archipelago. Air travel offers a unique viewpoint on this tropical paradise, whether you're traveling between far-off islands or just want to take in Vanuatu's splendor from above.

Trails for Walking and Biking

Explore Vanuatu's riding and walking routes to fully appreciate its natural beauty. Discover the calm trails that meander through verdant vistas, exposing undiscovered treasures and charming vantage points. Walking and bicycling routes provide a rejuvenating approach to getting to know the islands, whether you're a casual walker yearning for close interactions with nature or an expert biker searching out difficult terrains.

Vanuatu offers a variety of transportation alternatives, each of which opens a door to a distinct aspect of this tropical paradise. Let the variety of choices described in this chapter lead you on a tour of Vanuatu's landscapes, cultures, and hidden gems, regardless of your preference for the picturesque attractiveness of island hopping or the freedom of private transportation.

Visa and Entry Requirements

To guarantee a smooth entrance into this paradise, you must acquaint yourself with the visa and entry criteria before setting off on your trip to the tropical haven of Vanuatu. This chapter provides a comprehensive overview of the necessary paperwork, entrance requirements, and useful advice to ensure a stress-free arrival.

Visa Types

Vanuatu provides a variety of visas designed to meet different kinds of travel needs. Examine your alternatives; you may remain longer for those who want to do more exploring, or you can get a short-term tourist visa. Knowing the application procedure, costs, and any particular requirements related to each kind of visa will enable you to make well-informed judgments on the purpose and length of your stay.

Entry Documentation

Make sure you have all the required entrance paperwork in place as you get ready for your Vanuatu vacation. A thorough checklist covering documents including passports, letters of permission for visas, and any supplementary permits needed for certain activities is provided in this section. Ensure that your paperwork complies with Vanuatu's admission requirements to avoid any surprises down the road.

Application Process

Examine this section's step-by-step instructions to gain confidence while navigating the visa application procedure. Find out about the deadlines for applications, how to submit them, and if any supporting documentation is needed for a successful visa application. Knowing the procedure will help you be more prepared for a seamless admission into Vanuatu, regardless of whether you decide to apply online or via a diplomatic post.

Entry Regulations

Like any other location, Vanuatu has access restrictions in place to protect the health and safety of both tourists and locals. Read over these rules, paying particular attention to things like health standards, quarantine processes, and customs filings. Understanding admission requirements enables you to handle the arrival procedure responsibly and effectively.

Visa Extensions and Renewals

This section offers information about renewing and extending a visa for visitors who are captivated by

Vanuatu and would want to prolong their stay. Recognize the steps, deadlines, and prerequisites for extending your stay in this tropical haven. If the people, culture, or scenery enthrall you, understanding how to extend your visa will enable you to experience Vanuatu's delights to the fullest.

Tips for a Smooth Entry

Being well-prepared is essential for a stress-free entrance as a tourist. This section provides helpful advice on how to make sure your arrival in Vanuatu goes well. It covers topics like doing research before you arrive, interacting with local officials, and being aware of cultural quirks. Make the most of your trip by anticipating any problems and enjoying Vanuatu's friendly culture.

Armed with the knowledge of entrance and visa regulations, go off on your Vanuatu vacation with assurance. This chapter is your all-inclusive guide, making sure that all the paperwork and procedures perfectly match your vacation goals so you can concentrate on the beauty, tranquility, and cultural diversity this traveler's ideal location has to offer.

ISLAND ESSENTIALS

Weather and Climate

Bathed in tropical magnificence, Vanuatu has a climate that makes it an even more appealing year-round resort. An in-depth discussion of the weather patterns, seasonal variances, and climatic factors is provided in this chapter to assist you in making travel plans and maximizing the variety of experiences this archipelago has to offer.

Overview of Vanuatu's Climate

Explore a summary of the climate of Vanuatu, which is characterized by pleasant temperatures, mild trade breezes, and distinct wet and dry seasons. Recognize how the subtleties of this paradise's tropical environment affect everything from outdoor pursuits to cultural events. Vanuatu's environment suits a variety of tastes, whether you're a sun worshiper or would rather feel the soft touch of the wind.

Seasonal Variations

Discover how Vanuatu's scenery changes with the seasons all year long. Every season creates a different backdrop for your vacation experiences, from the dry season with its clear sky and perfect weather for water sports to the wet season with its rich flora and sporadic tropical rains. Learn about the benefits and things to think about while traveling at various seasons of the year so you can customize your trip to your tastes.

Best Times to Visit

Determine the ideal dates to visit Vanuatu depending on the activities you want to do and the kind of climate you want to have the greatest experience. This section walks you through the best months to enjoy bright festivals, peaceful beach days, or intensive wildlife discovery. Take into account how different weather conditions interact to create a customized travel schedule that suits your goals.

Packing Essentials

Make sure you pack appropriately for the temperature in Vanuatu as you get ready for your trip there. This section offers thorough packing advice, covering everything from lightweight, breathable textiles for warm days to waterproof clothes for infrequent tropical rains. Make sure you're adequately equipped for the many climates and activities that lie ahead so you can concentrate on Vanuatu's beauty without worrying about bad weather.

Tropical Weather Tips

By implementing these useful ideas into your travel routine, you can confidently navigate through tropical weather conditions. Find out how to remain hydrated, protect yourself from the sun, and enjoy the warmth without sacrificing comfort. These pointers guarantee that you enjoy every bit of Vanuatu's tropical appeal while being secure and well-prepared, whether you're shopping at outdoor markets, participating in water sports, or just lounging on the beach.

Climate's Influence on Activities

Recognize how the climate of Vanuatu affects the availability and scheduling of different activities. This section offers tips on coordinating your schedule with the islands' natural rhythms, from water activities that flourish in the sun to cultural events that spring to life during certain seasons.

Accept the balance between the weather and things to do to make your time in Vanuatu rewarding and well-rounded.

Prepare for the weather and climate of Vanuatu before you go there. This chapter acts as your weather compass, making sure that every moment in this tropical paradise is enhanced by the natural beauty that surrounds you, whether you're drawn to the vibrant festivals, the peace, and quiet of beach days, or the lush landscapes of the rainy season.

Language and Culture

Vanuatu is a mosaic of islands that is more than simply a place to visit; it's a fabric made of several languages and rich cultural traditions. To help you develop a greater understanding and respect for the people who live on these islands, this chapter encourages you to explore the colorful customs, diverse languages, and subtle cultural aspects that capture the spirit of Vanuatu.

Linguistic Diversity

Discover the variety of languages that make Vanuatu unique. This section introduces you to the most common languages and dialects spoken on the islands, where many different languages are spoken. The official language, Bislama, as well as indigenous languages spoken in certain areas, are examples of how knowing the linguistic landscape may improve your capacity to interact with people and fully immerse yourself in the culture.

Bislama: The National Language

Find out more about Bislama, the common language that unites Vanuatu's many linguistic groups. Learn about its history, idioms, and useful linguistic advice to get through everyday conversations. Learning a few Bislama phrases will enhance your cultural experience by facilitating conversation and creating a feeling of connection with the local population.

Cultural Traditions and Customs

Take a tour through the cultural traditions and customs of Vanuatu, where traditional ways of life combine with modern influences. Examine the meaning behind the dances, ceremonies, and rituals that are an essential aspect of everyday existence. Learn about traditional greetings, hand gestures, and clothing so that you may participate in Vanuatu's rich cultural history with respect.

Festivals and Celebrations

Take in the colorful excitement of Vanuatu's festivities and festivals. This section highlights the year's varied schedule of events, which ranges from exuberant music festivals to customary rituals. Festivals provide an insight into Vanuatu's radiant spirit, whether you're taking part in a yam festival, seeing traditional dances, or celebrating Independence Day.

Arts and Crafts

Discover the many forms of creative expression that exist in Vanuatu, ranging from elaborate traditional crafts to modern art scenes. Discover the artistry that goes into the beautifully carved objects, vivid paintings that depict the island culture, and woven mats. Learn how important art is to the Vanuatu people, and maybe take home a little piece of the archipelago's artistic heritage as a treasured keepsake.

Etiquette and Social Customs

Understand the norms and etiquette of the locals to successfully navigate social interactions while in

Vanuatu. Learn about the courteous gestures, eating manners, and communication standards that lead to pleasant and considerate interactions. By implementing these cultural insights into your encounters, you may embrace the warmth of Vanuatu's hospitality and create lasting relationships with the local population.

Cultural Sensitivity and Respect

This section highlights the value of cultural sensitivity and respect when you interact with Vanuatu's culture. Recognize the subtleties of mindfully engaging with local communities, attending rituals, and visiting holy locations. In addition to improving your personal experience, adopting cultural awareness helps to preserve and recognize Vanuatu's distinctive legacy.

Set off on a cultural journey through Vanuatu, a place where customs and language blend to provide a rich tapestry of experiences. This chapter is your cultural map, taking you through the subtle language differences and varied practices that make Vanuatu a place where every encounter turns into a meaningful conversation and where every display of culture offers a window into the essence of the islands.

Money and Banking

Vanuatu's distinctive currency system and banking infrastructure are the beating heart of the country's economy. This chapter walks you through the practical issues of handling your money while traveling, so you may confidently and easily negotiate the economic terrain of the islands.

Vanuatu's Currency: Vatu

Learn about the Vatu, the national currency of Vanuatu. Discover what makes the Vatu distinctive, including their history, denominations, and characteristics. Understanding currency conversion rates is made easier with the help of this section, which will help you determine how much the Vatu is worth about your native currency. Being knowledgeable about money matters enables you to make smart financial choices that fit within your trip budget, whether you're utilizing ATMs or local banks for currency exchange.

Banking Facilities

Examine the banking options on each of the islands that make up Vanuatu. An overview of nearby banks, their offerings, and the locations of ATMs is given in this section. Knowing the state of the banking industry will guarantee that you have easy and safe ways to manage your money, regardless of whether you need to make cash withdrawals, currency exchanges, or other financial activities while traveling.

Currency Exchange Tips

Utilize useful advice while navigating currency conversion to get the most out of your money. This section gives you the information you need to make wise selections, from locating exchange places that are advantageous to comprehending possible expenses. These pointers guarantee that you make the most of your financial transactions while taking in Vanuatu's natural splendor, whether you're exchanging money at banks, lodging facilities, or neighborhood exchange offices.

Credit Cards and Payment Methods

Examine if credit cards and other payment options are accepted across Vanuatu. Find out which businesses take credit cards more easily and which ones would prefer cash purchases. This segment offers valuable perspectives on the benefits and factors to take into account for various payment options, guaranteeing a smooth and safe transaction experience for you when making purchases or payments along your trip.

Budgeting for Your Vanuatu Adventure

Creating a budget is a crucial step in the vacation preparation process. This section walks you through creating a budget for your Vanuatu trip, taking into account the cost of lodging, transportation, food, and activities. get sure you get the most out of your trip without sacrificing your financial peace of mind by customizing your budget to fit your travel tastes and style.

Managing Finances Responsibly

Encourage prudent money management throughout your trip to Vanuatu. The significance of responsible spending, encouraging local companies, and promoting sustainable tourism is emphasized in this section. In addition to improving your personal travel experience, prudent money management also benefits the local economy and communities.

With the information necessary to understand the financial and monetary systems of the islands, go out on your Vanuatu adventure with assurance. As your financial manual, this chapter will help you manage your money sensibly and easily so that you may enjoy Vanuatu's marvels.

EXPLORING REGIONS

North Shore: Pristine Beaches and Water Activities

With its spotless beaches, glistening seas, and a plethora of water sports, Vanuatu's North Shore entices visitors with the promise of an aquatic paradise. This chapter allows you to discover the captivating coastal attractions, from quiet beaches to exhilarating water sports, and to weave memories along the northern coasts of this tropical paradise.

Introducing the North Shore

Travel to the North Shore, where white sand beaches and blue seas meld together harmoniously. An overview of the region's geography is given in this part, emphasizing the variety of landscapes that are just waiting to be discovered. The North Shore provides the ideal environment for a memorable seaside experience, whether you're looking for peace on remote beaches or exciting water sports.

Secluded Beaches and Hidden Coves

Explore the charm of isolated coves and beaches dotted around the North Shore. This area reveals the hidden treasures that provide peace, from unspoiled beaches to secluded coves surrounded by thick flora. The North Shore's secret beaches welcome you to relax and take in Vanuatu's natural beauty, whether you're a nature lover, a sun worshiper, or someone looking for a peaceful getaway.

Water Activities Paradise

Give yourself up to a universe of water sports that make the North Shore seem like a floating paradise. This area presents a range of possibilities, suitable for both thrill-seekers and those who prefer more relaxed activities. Divers of all skill levels may enjoy a variety of water activities on the North Shore, including kayaking along scenic beaches and snorkeling in vivid coral reefs.

Snorkeling and Diving Hotspots

Explore the North Shore's underwater attractions, which include colorful coral reefs brimming with marine life. Discover well-known locations for diving and snorkeling, each providing a unique window into the abundant wildlife below the surface. The underwater scenery of the North Shore offers an enthralling dive or snorkeling experience for novices alike, welcoming you into Vanuatu's aquatic world.

Beachfront Dining and Relaxation

Enjoy the delights of Vanuatu's food while admiring breathtaking views of the beach. This section directs you to beachside restaurants where you may savor worldwide cuisine and regional specialties while listening to the soothing sound of the waves and the soft sea wind. The North Shore's culinary options complement your beach experience, whether you're having a laid-back lunch on the beach or a romantic supper under the stars.

Sunset Strolls and Coastal Retreats

Take strolls along the scenic coasts of the North Shore as the sun sets on your days. Find beachside hideaways that provide the ideal blend of leisure and scenic beauty. This area helps you find the perfect places to stay so you can relax and experience the peace of the North Shore, from isolated resorts to boutique beachside lodging.

Responsible Tourism and Conservation Efforts

Discover the North Shore's environmental initiatives to embrace the spirit of responsible tourism. Initiatives to protect the area's marine ecosystems and natural beauty are highlighted in this section. By helping to preserve the North Shore, you can make sure that its unspoiled beauty is retained for future generations, whether you take part in community-led initiatives or just follow the rules of responsible beach etiquette.

Set off on a journey around the North Shore's coastline, where you can enjoy a multitude of water sports and immaculate beaches. This chapter invites you to immerse yourself in the beauty, adventure, and tranquility that characterize Vanuatu's northern coasts, acting as your guide to a seaside sanctuary.

Central Highlands: Hiking Trails and Nature Reserves

With its patchwork of green valleys, rich sceneries, and strenuous hiking paths, Vanuatu's Central Highlands lure nature lovers and adventure seekers. Discover the wild splendor of the highlands in this chapter, which offers hiking trails and wildlife preserves showcasing the rich biodiversity of this fascinating area.

Accepting the Highlands of Central

Travel to the center of the Central Highlands of Vanuatu, a paradise for outdoor enthusiasts with its undulating hills and thick woods. The region's physical and biological characteristics are introduced in this part, laying the groundwork for an engrossing investigation of its nature reserves and hiking routes.

Trails for Hiking at Every Level

Explore a variety of hiking routes suitable for all skill levels, from novices to experienced trekkers. The Central Highlands provide a range of routes that let you experience nature at your speed, whether you're looking for a leisurely walk through picturesque landscapes or a strenuous climb to panoramic overlooks.

Highland Plant and Animal Life

Discover the Central Highlands' abundant biodiversity, which includes a wide variety of fauna and natural plant species. This section offers an overview of the several ecosystems that you will come across on the hiking paths, as well as a peek at the colorful flora and creatures that live in the highlands. As you walk these trails rich in natural features, don't forget to bring binoculars for birding and an acute eye for endemic species.

Conservation Areas and Nature Reserves

Investigate the protected nature reserves and conservation areas that are essential to maintaining the Central Highlands' natural integrity. This section takes you to places where conservation efforts are flourishing, from immaculate wilderness regions to well-maintained reserves. Find out about the current efforts and projects that support the preservation of the natural heritage of the highlands.

Beautiful Views and Waterfalls

Set off on an adventure to see spectacular views and tumbling waterfalls tucked away in the Central Highlands. This part takes you to some of the most picturesque locations on the hiking trails, where the tranquility of waterfalls and expansive vistas provide an enthralling setting for your outdoor experiences. These natural treasures are waiting for you to discover them, whether your goal is to take the ideal shot or just to take in the splendor.

Tours with guides and educational programs

With informative programs and guided tours conducted by experienced local guides, you can make the most of your time in the Central Highlands. This section looks at ways to participate in nature walks, guided treks, and educational programs that provide a greater understanding of the ecological and cultural importance of the highlands. Talk to knowledgeable locals who are as passionate about the area's natural resources as you are.

Lodging in the Highland Region

Discover lodgings that provide the ideal balance of comfort and closeness to nature, tucked away in the Central Highlands. Whether your preference is for cozy guesthouses, environmentally conscious hotels, or immersive stays within nature reserves, this section directs you to lodging options that will enhance your hiking experience and make sure you have a smooth and peaceful stay in the highlands.

In Vanuatu's Central Highlands, on a hiking and nature discovery adventure the wild beauty of the area is revealed at every turn. This chapter invites you to immerse yourself in the tranquility of the highlands by acting as your trailhead to a world of verdant landscapes, varied ecosystems, and exhilarating outdoor excursions.

East Coast: Cultural Heritage and Local Cuisine

Vanuatu's East Coast offers a mesmerizing fusion of gastronomic pleasures and cultural diversity. This chapter allows you to discover the rich tapestry of customs, historical landmarks, and mouthwatering regional food that characterize the East Coast's cultural legacy.

East Coast Cultural Heritage

Take in the East Coast's rich cultural legacy, where history and customs converge to form an engrossing tale. You will learn about historical monuments, cultural landmarks, and customs that highlight the distinctive character of the coastal villages in this part. The East Coast welcomes you to explore its diverse cultural fabric, which includes both contemporary festivities and age-old rites.

Historical Sites and Landmarks

Discover the history of the East Coast by visiting the historical monuments and landmarks that adorn the area. This segment leads you through historically significant locations, from colonial ruins to indigenous cultural sites, letting you discover the narratives woven throughout the landscapes of the East Coast. Explore historical towns, museums, and heritage sites to learn more about the development of the local culture.

Conventional Crafts and Arts

Explore the East Coast's thriving traditional arts and crafts, where talented craftspeople are preserving and showcasing their rich cultural legacy. This part exposes you to the artistry that goes into creating traditional artworks, wood sculptures, and intricately woven fabrics. Discover how these cultural gems are made by visiting neighborhood markets and artisan workshops. You may even be able to carry home a piece of the East Coast's creative heritage.

Festivals & Cultural Events

Take in the colorful excitement of the festivals and cultural events that line the East Coast's schedule. Whether it's a folk dance show, a music festival, or an event honoring regional traditions, this section reveals the wide range of events that let you experience the festive vibe of the area. If you want to experience real culture, schedule your vacation around these events.

Regional Cuisine: East Coast Flavors

Take a gastronomic tour of the East Coast's delicacies, where regional food reflects the variety of the area's cultures. The traditional recipes, locally sourced ingredients, and distinctive cooking techniques that characterize the cuisine of the East Coast are introduced to you in this part. Savor the flavors that make East Coast cuisine a delectable study of Vanuatu's culinary history, from fragrant spices to fresh seafood.

Dining Out with Local Restaurants

Discover local restaurants and dining experiences that highlight the greatest food from the East Coast. This section directs you to places that provide a true flavor of the area, whether you're enjoying a seafood feast on the beach or traditional drinks in a little café. Talk to regional cooks and enjoy the warmth that comes with every meal.

Workshops & Experiences in Culinary Arts

Enrich your understanding of East Coast cooking by taking part in classes and events. Opportunities to explore indigenous ingredients, pick up traditional cooking techniques, and participate in practical culinary activities are highlighted in this area. Take in the East Coast's culinary talents and create unforgettable events that combine learning with delicious food.

Set off on a gastronomic and cultural journey around the East Coast, where customs, history, and regional cuisine combine to provide a deep and engaging experience. This chapter is your tour guide to the culinary delights and rich cultural legacy of Vanuatu's eastern coast.

South Islands: Relaxation and Secluded Retreats

Vanuatu's South Islands provide a peaceful sanctuary where leisure blends with the scenic splendor of isolated hideouts. This chapter encourages you to explore the tranquil settings, undiscovered adventures, and restorative encounters that characterize the southern archipelago's appeal.

The South Islands' Serenity

Travel to the South Islands, where peaceful coves, immaculate beaches, and verdant surroundings await you. To prepare you for a healing and revitalizing stay in this southern paradise, this section will expose you to the geographical elements that contribute to the peaceful ambiance.

Private Getaways and Lodging

Find quiet havens and lodgings tucked away in the South Islands' central region. This section points you in the direction of hidden treasures that provide the ideal balance of comfort and isolation, whether you're looking for an eco-friendly resort, a beachfront home, or an overwater cottage. Savor the seclusion and calm provided by these unique sanctuaries as you take in the breathtaking natural beauty of the South Islands.

Flawless Shorelines and Coastal Paradise

Savor the pure beaches and tranquility along the shore that characterize the South Islands. This part reveals the hidden locations where you may relax, take in the sun, and listen to the soft sound of the waves—from unexplored shorelines to secluded coves. The South Islands provide a canvas of coastal tranquility, whether you're strolling down the seashore or relaxing on the sand.

Spa and Wellbeing Experiences

Enhance your journey of relaxation with wellness and spa treatments that are intended to revive the body, mind, and spirit. You will learn about spa resorts and wellness facilities in this area that combine conventional medical procedures with contemporary amenities. Treat yourself to therapeutic massages, yoga classes, and holistic therapies, and let the South Islands turn into a haven for your health.

Eco-Experiences and Nature Retreats

Take part in eco-experiences and environment retreats that showcase the South Islands' biodiversity and natural beauties. This area leads you through possibilities to engage with the pure environment, such as guided nature walks and birding expeditions. Take part in environmentally friendly activities that have little effect on the fragile ecosystems of the southern archipelago and learn about local conservation initiatives.

Gourmet Treats in Private

Savor delicious food in quiet settings where the regional tastes of the South Islands are brought to life. This section exposes you to gourmet experiences that highlight the area's culinary prowess, as well as seaside dining and private picnics. Savor international cuisine, fresh seafood, and tropical fruits while taking in the stunning seascapes.

Beachside Recreation and Activities

Take part in beachside recreation and activities that enhance the South Islands' relaxed vibe. Enjoy the slow-paced activities that let you truly appreciate island life—kayaking in serene lagoons, paddleboarding along the coast, or just lounging by the ocean. This section walks you through all of these options.

Set off on a voyage of rest and renewal in the South Islands, where isolated hideaways and breathtaking scenery form a peaceful refuge. This chapter is your road map to the tranquil settings, undiscovered adventures, and restorative activities that await you in Vanuatu's southern regions.

ACCOMMODATIONS

With its captivating archipelago, Vanuatu provides a variety of lodging choices to suit every taste and price range of visitors. Vanuatu welcomes you to embark on a stay that suits your travel objectives, whether you want the elegance of luxury resorts, the charm of boutique hotels, the affordability of budget-friendly stays, or the novelty of unorthodox lodgings.

Luxurious Resorts: Extravagance Among the Canvas of Nature

The luxurious resorts of Vanuatu reinvent the art of extravagance by skillfully fusing extravagance with the surrounding breathtaking scenery. These resorts, which provide luxurious overwater bungalows and beachfront villas, are the pinnacle of elegance and leisure.

Overwater Elegance: Envision yourself sitting over pristine turquoise seas in a private overwater home. Vanuetu's luxury resorts specialize in providing these exquisite suites, which have individual decks with direct access to the water. Enjoy unbroken views of the dawn breaking the horizon as you wake up to the soft sound of breaking waves.

Spa Sanctuaries: World-class spas at many opulent resorts in Vanuatu reinvent what it means to unwind. Rejuvenate yourself with treatments modeled after traditional island cures while taking in views of the tranquil ocean or verdant gardens. Allow knowledgeable therapists to treat you using organic materials and holistic techniques to guarantee a peaceful getaway from the worries of the outside world.

Gourmet Experiences: The upscale resorts in Vanuatu provide a plethora of delectable dishes in their gourmet restaurants. Skilled chefs create dishes that highlight both regional specialties and global cuisine, often accompanied by excellent wines and stunning views of the ocean. Savor eating al fresco on the beach, where each occasion turns into a celebration of Vanuatu's delectable cuisine.

Exclusive Activities: In addition to providing opulent lodging, luxury resorts offer their visitors unique experiences. These resorts make sure that every moment is customized to your preferences, offering anything from guided underwater adventures to private boat charters. Immerse yourself in the colorful underwater world, take a helicopter trip, or just relax on your private beach—the options are as limitless as the sea itself.

Boutique Hotels: Personal Touches in Every Element

Vanuatu's boutique hotels are a delightful substitute for bigger resorts for those who value individualized service and distinctive character. These cozy, stylish, and personal lodgings let you fully experience the local way of life.

Creative Ambiance: Vanuatu's boutique hotels often include unique design features that capture the islands' creative spirit. Anticipate locally produced furniture, striking artwork, and well-chosen interiors that express the destination's narrative. Every boutique stay is an homage to the originality and genuineness that characterize Vanuatu's way of life.

Local Immersion: You feel the warmth of the community's friendliness as soon as you enter a boutique hotel. These lodgings often place a high value on fostering relationships with the local community by providing chances to interact with craftspeople, go to cultural events, or just enjoy home-cooked meals that highlight Vanuatu's distinctive cuisine.

Personalized Service: Because boutique hotels are small and private, staff members can provide personalized service and often know customers by name. Your stay will seem more personalized because of the staff's attention to detail, which extends to setting up customized tours, pointing out hidden treasures, and making sure dietary requirements are satisfied.

Charming Locations: Boutique hotels are often tucked away in charming locations that provide a feeling of privacy and calm. Savor views of beautiful gardens, unwind in secret courtyards, or choose a hillside refuge with sweeping views of the surroundings. Every boutique accommodation is a peaceful sanctuary that invites you to relax and enjoy the slower tempo of island living.

Low-Cost Accommodations: Inexpensive Amenities with Island Feel

Vanuatu offers a selection of lodging options that provide reasonable conveniences without sacrificing the authenticity of the island experience for those on a tight budget. These reasonably priced accommodations meet a range of demands, so every visitor may experience Vanuatu without going over budget.

Guesthouses and Homestays: Choose one of these lodging options to feel the true warmth of Vanuatuan hospitality. These lodgings provide comfortable rooms and an opportunity to interact with neighborhood families, giving visitors a genuine look at daily life on the island. Savor freshly prepared meals and tailored suggestions for visiting the area.

Hostels & Dormitories: Hostels and dormitories in Vanuatu provide affordable lodging alternatives and are perfect for lone travelers or those looking for a communal environment. After a day of island discovery, enjoy the simplicity of a cozy bed and the company of other tourists as you exchange tales in the common areas.

Local Hotels & Inns: Vanuatu's local hotels and inns provide basic, reasonably priced lodging with all the necessities. These reasonably priced lodging options, which are spread out around the archipelago, provide a useful starting point for island exploration.

Self-Catering Apartments: Self-catering apartments are an affordable option for anyone who would want a more autonomous stay. Savor the freedom to plan your schedule at your speed and the flexibility of cooking your meals with fresh, local items. You may live like a local and enjoy a cozy environment in these flats in Vanuatu.

Unusual Lodging Experiences: Exceeding Standard Stays

Additionally, Vanuatu provides unusual and distinctive lodging options that guarantee a visit unlike any other. These unconventional choices, which vary from daring treehouse stays to eco-friendly resorts, guarantee an unforgettable trip.

Treehouse Escapes: Spend a night in a treehouse surrounded by the verdant scenery of Vanuatu to embrace your inner explorer. Enjoy treetop vistas while unplugging technology and getting back in touch with the natural world. The sound of rustling leaves and songbirds will envelop you.

Eco-Friendly Retreats: Select eco-friendly retreats that emphasize environmental conservation to align your visit with sustainable practices. By using waste minimization techniques, renewable energy sources, and local sourcing, these lodgings often let you take in Vanuatu's natural beauty with the least amount of environmental impact possible.

Underwater Accommodations: Immerse yourself in a one-of-a-kind encounter by selecting lodging that allows you to get up close and personal with the thriving aquatic environment that surrounds Vanuatu. Imagine having a dreamlike and remarkable stay as you doze off to the captivating dance of fish right outside your windows.

Staying in traditional villages allows you to fully immerse yourself in Vanuatu's rich cultural history. Take part in traditional ceremonies, feel the coziness of community life, and learn about ancient customs. These stays with cultural immersion provide a deep connection to the local way of life.

Creating Your Own Vanuatu Experience: A Personalized Tour

Vanuatu guarantees that your stay will be as varied and fascinating as its archipelago, regardless of your preference for the opulent luxuries of luxury resorts, the cozy charms of boutique hotels, the affordability of budget-friendly stays, or the novelty of unusual lodgings. By selecting lodging that complements your way of travel, you can tailor your Vanuatu experience and weave memories rich in comfort, culture, and unspoiled beauty.

CULINARY DELIGHTS

Traditional Vanuatu Dishes

The rich cultural legacy and abundant land and marine resources of the archipelago of Vanuatu are reflected in the gastronomic landscape, which is a lively tapestry. This chapter delves into the essence of Vanuatuan cuisine, highlighting classic dishes that entice the taste buds and provide a fascinating gastronomic tour across the islands.

1. Lap

Description: A typical Vanuatuan delicacy called Lap highlights the creativity of regional culinary customs. It's made of grated root vegetables (usually taro or yams) combined with coconut cream, wrapped in banana leaf, and baked until it has a nice, crispy texture. Additions like meat, fish, or vegetables may be included to create variations that give a flexible cuisine that suits a variety of palates.

Serving Suggestion: During festive occasions, get-togethers with family, and cultural festivals, a lap is often served as the main meal. The dish's overall attractiveness is enhanced by the faint earthy taste that the banana leaf wrapping adds to it.

2. Palusami

Description: Palusami is a meal that perfectly captures the tastes of Vanuatu. It has fresh taro leaves with onions, garlic, and sometimes fish or meat mixed with thick coconut cream. After the combination is perfectly cooked and wrapped in banana leaves, a rich, savory meal with a creamy texture is produced.

Serving Suggestion: Palusami is a popular dish that is often served at feasts and special occasions. It is a valued and soothing component of Vanuatu cuisine, thanks to its fragrant combination of taro and coconut leaves.

3. Coconut Crab

Description: The Coconut Crab is a specialty of Vanuatu known for its distinct flavor and large size. Usually cooked in its shell, this giant land crab brings out the delicacy of its delicious flesh. Vanuatu's abundant coastal resources are exemplified by Coconut Crab, a culinary gem that's often cooked with coconut milk and indigenous seasonings.

Serving Suggestion: Serve Coconut Crab as the star of a seafood feast or as a main course on celebratory occasions. Vanuatu's characteristics are embodied in the delicious sensation created by the richness of coconut and the soft, sweet flesh.

4. **Bougna Vanuetuan**

Description: Bougna is a classic feast meal from Vanuatu that perfectly captures the essence of group cooking. It entails wrapping a mixture of root vegetables, coconut milk, and meat—typically chicken or fish—in banana leaves. After that, the package is baked in an earth oven, giving the contents a smokey, earthy flavor.

Serving Suggestion: Bougna is often made for special occasions, family get-togethers, and cultural festivals. In Vanuetuan tradition, the communal nature of its preparation and sharing makes it a symbol of unity.

5. **Nasara**

Description: The native Vanuetuan dessert known as Nasara honors the islands' abundant supply of sweets. It is made out of ripe bananas or plantains that are often deep-fried till crispy and golden. The perfect balance of sweetness and crunch is achieved by drizzling honey or coconut syrup over the fried bananas.

Serving Suggestion: Nasara is a well-liked dessert that is consumed during festivals, celebrations, and informal get-togethers. Both residents and tourists like this snack because of its sweetness and simplicity.

6. Tropical Fruit Salad

Description: The Vanuatuan Fruit Salad is a delightful combination of tropical fruits that highlights the wide range of tastes present in the area. A common combination of ingredients is pineapple, mango, papaya, and coconut, which is sometimes augmented with a dash of lime or passion fruit juice.

Serving Suggestion: This fruit salad goes well as a light dessert after a filling dinner or as a side dish on a sunny day. Vanuatu's natural sweetness and vivid hues perfectly capture the spirit of the tropics.

7. Ika Mata

Description: A popular Vanuetuan meal that showcases the freshness of the fish in the area is called Ika Mata. It usually comprises raw fish marinated in lime or lemon juice, coconut cream, and fish (usually tuna or barracuda). Onions, tomatoes, and chile are used to flavor the meal, giving it a delicious and zesty taste.

Serving Suggestion: Ika Mata is a well-liked light dinner or appetizer that is ideal for anyone who wants to sample some of Vanuatu's abundant seaside cuisine. On warm island days, its zesty and refreshing flavor profile makes it a pleasant option.

Accept the Flavors of Vanuatu

Fresh, regional ingredients and generation-old cooking customs are celebrated in Vanuatu cuisine. Vanuatu's traditional meals encourage you to experience the distinct aromas that characterize this wonderful island, from celebratory feasts to daily joys. Every taste is a voyage into the core of Vanuatuan culture and cuisine, whether you're relishing the sweetness of Nasara or the richness of Lap Lap.

Dining Hotspots

Set out on a gastronomic journey around Vanuatu as we investigate the popular eateries that entice you to sample the many cuisines of this captivating archipelago with a symphony of aromas.

1. Seaside Elegance: Coral Breeze Restaurant

- *Location:* Port Vila, Efate
- *Ambiance:* With sweeping views of the ocean in front of it, Coral Breeze Restaurant provides a classy dining experience overlooking the turquoise waves. The casual furnishings and outdoor location combine to create a subtle elegance.
- *Cuisine:* Savor a cuisine of the freshest seafood Vanuatu has to offer, with dishes like Grilled Mahi-Mahi and Coconut Crab Bisque. The culinary team creates a

gastronomic experience that reflects the variety of the archipelago by deftly fusing regional foods with inspirations from across the world.

2. Cultural Fusion: Tanna Spice Kitchen

- *Location:* Tanna Island's Lenakel
- *Ambiance:* Let yourself get carried away by Tanna Spice Kitchen's vivid hues and friendly greetings. To provide a warm environment where patrons may engage with the island's rich cultural legacy, this dining destination expertly combines traditional Vanuatuan design with contemporary comfort.
- *Cuisine:* Tanna Spice Kitchen is renowned for combining regional cuisines with global influences. Savor the delectable Yasur Volcano Pepper Steak or Tanna Taro Gnocchi, which pays respect to the island's fiery volcanic scenery.

3. Coconut Grove Restaurant Exudes Island Charm

- *Location:* Espiritu Santo, Luganville

- *Ambiance:* Coconut Grove Restaurant radiates island charm and tranquility as it is tucked away within beautiful tropical grounds. A tranquil and relaxed ambiance is created by the open-air seating, which lets patrons eat in the shadow of swaying palm palms.
- *Cuisine:* Savor delectable dishes influenced by the abundant sea and land of Espiritu Santo. From Grilled Lobster Tails to Vanuetuan Bougna, the cuisine embodies the spirit of the island's savory and fresh ingredients.

4. Feels of the Past: The Old French House

- *Location:* Efate's Port Vila
- *Ambiance:* The Old French House, which is housed in a gorgeous edifice from the colonial period, offers guests to go back in time while enjoying modern cuisine. An unforgettable eating experience is produced by the vintage atmosphere and antique furnishings.
- *Cuisine:* The Old French House prides itself on serving only the freshest, regional ingredients on its menu. Savor meals with a hint of historical grandeur, such as Coconut

Panna Cotta flavored with tropical tastes or Bouillabaisse made with shrimp from Vanuatu.

5. **Restaurant Blue Lagoon: Beachfront Bliss**

- *Location:* Efate
- *Ambiance:* Blue Lagoon Restaurant provides a charming, toes-in-the-sand beachside eating experience. It is located along the coasts of Efate. Diners may have a delicious dinner while taking in the splendor of Vanuatu's seaside views in this laid-back atmosphere.
- *Cuisine:* Savor a wide selection of dishes including wood-fired pizzas, fruit drinks, and seafood platters with an island flair. It's the ideal location for romantic evenings beneath the stars or leisurely lunches because of the laid-back vibe.

6. **Market-to-Table Freshness: Port Olry Beachfront Cafe**

- *Location:* Espiritu Santo's Port Olry
- *Ambience:* With a rustic, bohemian vibe, this beachside café overlooks the immaculate Port Olry Beach. The calm setting for a

relaxed and private eating experience is created by the simple timber furniture and the sound of the waves breaking close.

- *Cuisine:* Fresh vegetables purchased straight from the neighborhood market are a source of pride for Port Olry Beachfront Cafe. Savor foods like Grilled Pineapple Chicken and Coconut Lime Prawns, are made with an emphasis on highlighting Vanuatu's natural tastes.

7. Le Flamboyant Restaurant: A Mountain Retreat

- *Location:* Tanna Island's Mount Yasur
- *Ambiance:* Le Flamboyant Restaurant, which is perched atop Mount Yasur, provides stunning views of the surrounding volcanic landscapes. Diners may enjoy their food outside while taking in the enchantment of Tanna's natural beauties.
- *Cuisine:* To provide a varied gastronomic experience, the menu combines foreign and Vanuetuan delicacies. To experience the distinct tastes influenced by the volcanic landscape of the island, try the Tanna Taro Pancakes or the Volcano Stone-Grilled Steak.

8. Enjoyment on the Riverside: Riri Blue Hole Bar & Restaurant

- *Location:* Efate
- *Ambiance:* Riri Blue Hole Bar & Restaurant is a calm haven from the bustle, nestled next to a placid river and surrounded by verdant foliage. The riverbank seating and rustic décor make for a perfect backdrop for a quiet dinner.
- *Cuisine:* Savor a meal that highlights the finest seafood and land offerings from Vanuatu. The meals, which range from Grilled Venison to River Prawn Pasta, showcase a dedication to ecological procedures and local sourcing, offering a lovely dining experience by the river.

Culinary Memories Await

Vanuatu's cuisine is so varied that every restaurant you visit opens a new door to the many tastes that make up this fascinating archipelago. Savor the gastronomic gems that lie at Vanuatu's dining havens, from coastal pleasure to elegant seaside dining.

Street Food Adventures

Vanuatu's thriving street food scene entices you to go on a gastronomic adventure where mouthwatering smells, smoldering grills, and busy market stalls come together to create a lovely mosaic of sidewalk treats. This chapter delves into the vibrant streets and neighborhood markets where street food is elevated to a celebration of Vanuatuan cuisine.

1. **Market Morsels: Port Vila Municipal Market**

- *Location:* Efate's Port Vila

Highlights:

- *Coconut Crab Samosas:* A delicious combination of the well-known coconut crab and spices influenced by India, encased in a crispy samosa shell.
- *Fresh Fruit Skewers:* A colorful snack ideal for a light meal, these skewers include tropical fruits including papaya, mango, and pineapple.

Experience: Wander around the vibrant Port Vila Municipal Market booths, where regional sellers provide a wide selection of street foods. Interact with vendors, try the seasonal products in the market, and take in the vibrant ambiance of this food center.

2. Beachside Bites: Erakor Beach Fish & Chips Stand

Location: Efate's Erakor Beach

Highlights:

- *Grilled Tuna Tacos:* Freshly grilled tuna topped with crunchy veggies and a zesty lime dressing are served on soft tortillas as Grilled Tuna Tacos.
- *Coconut Crusted Prawns:* A delicious combination of textures, and succulent prawns covered in a crunchy coconut crust.

Experience: Take a stroll down Erakor Beach and uncover this fish and chips stand's hidden treasure. Enjoy the tastes of Vanuatu's coastal richness in a laid-back seaside atmosphere with the sound of waves lapping against the sand under your feet.

3. Luxurious Dusk: The Port Vila Night Market

Location: Efate's Port Vila

Highlights:

- *Vanuetuan BBQ Skewers:* Vanuatuan BBQ Skewers are skewers loaded with marinated meats that are perfectly cooked and flavored with smokey and fragrant spices.
- *Taro Fritters:* A favorite local staple, these crispy fritters are created from shredded taro and come with a side of zesty dipping sauce.

Experience: Visit Port Vila Night Market as the sun sets to take in the tantalizing smells of street cuisine and the sizzle of grills. Take part in the vibrant evening atmosphere with the locals and indulge in a variety of savory and sweet delights.

4. **Mele Cascades Fruit Stand: A Rural Bounty**

Location: Mele, Efate

Highlights:

- *Pawpaw Salsa Cups:* Fresh pawpaw stuffed with a fiery salsa created from regional ingredients including tomatoes, onions, and chili is known as Pawpaw Salsa Cups.

- *Yam Chips with Coconut Dip:* A delicious combination of sweet and earthy tastes, crispy yam chips, and creamy coconut dip.

Experience: To get a sense of rural Vanuatu, go to Mele Cascades Fruit Stand. This street food paradise, surrounded by beautiful vegetation, lets you enjoy the simplicity and purity of tastes created from the abundant products of the islands.

5. **Hillside Delights: Tanna Roots & Yams Supplier**

Location: Tanna Island's Mount Yasur

Highlights:

- *Roasted Tanna Yams:* Yams produced nearby, expertly roasted, and garnished with a dash of sea salt.
- *Cassava Pops:* Tiny cassava nibbles with a delightful crunch that are deep-fried till golden brown.

Experience: Savor the earthy deliciousness of yams and roots from street sellers as you stroll up Mount

Yasur's slopes. Savor these filling and healthy delicacies while taking in the breathtaking views of the volcanic landscapes.

6. Hidden Gem: Luganville Local Snack Stalls

Location: Espiritu Santo, Luganville

Highlights:

- *Nakamal Platter:* An extensive introduction to Vanuatu cuisine, this platter includes local specialties including lap, palusami, and coconut crab.
- *Mango Sticky Rice:* A delicious tropical delicacy made with sweet, sticky rice, juicy mango segments, and coconut cream poured over.

Experience: Wander through Luganville's winding streets, where tucked-away snack stands reveal a wealth of delicious Vanuatu cuisine. Talk to the people, sample the variety of options, and find the hidden gastronomic treasures that make this place a veritable sanctuary for street food lovers.

Savoring Sidewalk Stories

Every meal you have while exploring Vanuatu's streets becomes a new chapter in the islands' extensive culinary history. Street food excursions in Vanuatu, from market stalls to seaside sellers, offer not only a feast for the senses but also an insight into the character and heart of this enchanted island.

ACTIVITIES AND EXCURSIONS

Water Sports and Marine Adventures

Water lovers may enjoy a wide range of exhilarating sports in Vanuatu's aquatic playground, which is enhanced by the island's immaculate seas and abundant marine life. This chapter delves into the thrilling world of water sports and marine exploration, which entices travelers to discover the surface and depths of Vanuatu's turquoise waters.

1. Swimming at the Blue Lagoon

Location: Efate

Experience: Snorkeling at Blue Lagoon is a captivating experience due to its pristine seas. Explore below the surface to find a rainbow of coral reefs brimming with vibrant aquatic life. Explore this underwater paradise and come across colorful coral formations, clownfish, and parrotfish.

Advice: For a better understanding of the marine environment, think about taking a guided snorkeling excursion and using eco-friendly sunscreen.

2. At Million Dollar Point, Scuba Diving

Location: Espiritu Santo, Luganville

Experience: Take a plunge into history at Million Dollar Point, an underwater archaeological site that was abandoned after World War II and has a vast array of military hardware, including tanks, jeeps, and machinery covered in coral. This unusual diving spot offers adventurers a look into the island's history during the conflict.

Advice: For a more thorough experience, make sure your diving certification is current, and think about hiring a local dive guide.

3. Kayaking over the River Riri Riri

Location: Efate

Experience: Take a kayaking excursion in the Riri Riri River's mild currents. Paddle through verdant mangrove trees while taking in the peace and seeing a variety of bird species. Select a tandem kayak or a solo kayak for a cooperative expedition.

Advice: For the best weather, start your kayaking adventure in the early morning or late afternoon. Don't forget to use sunscreen and a hat.

4. Surfing at Pango Point

Location: Efate

Experience: Consistent waves that suit both novice and expert surfers may be found at Pango Point, a surfing paradise. Take a rental surfboard, ride the waves along this gorgeous beach, and catch the swells. The thrill of surfing amid Vanuatu's breathtaking scenery is a once-in-a-lifetime opportunity.

Advice: If you're new to surfing, take a class and observe the customs of the local surf community.

5. Whale Watching off Tanna's Coast

Location: Tanna Island

Experience: Head out on a whale-watching excursion near Tanna, where Vanuatu's seas are home to humpback whale migrations. See these magnificent animals breach and play in their natural environment, producing a scene that inspires both wonder and respect.

Advice: Choose a reliable whale-watching excursion and maintain a polite distance from the aquatic animals.

6. **Stand-Up Paddleboarding in Havannah Harbour**

Location: Efate

Experience: Take a stand-up paddleboard (SUP) and glide over the serene waves of Havannah Harbour. Take in the tranquility of the port as it is surrounded by pristine blue sky and verdant hills. SUP is a great method to experience the visual grandeur of Vanuatu's coastal surroundings in addition to being a soothing hobby.

Advice: Wear a leash for safety while paddleboarding, and choose a quiet day.

7. **Game Fishing in Vanuatu's Waters**

Location: Multiple places

Experience: Game fish including mahi-mahi, tuna, and marlin abound in Vanuatu's seas. Take part in a game fishing trip to push your fishing limits and experience the excitement of landing a large catch. Engaging in deep-sea fishing excursions offers a chance to experience the abundance of the ocean.

Advice: Reserve a fishing charter with knowledgeable captains, and be ready for an action-packed day out on the ocean.

8. Jet Skiing along Mele Bay

Location: Efate

Experience: Mele Bay provides an excellent jet skiing environment where you can race across the sea, explore the shoreline, and get an adrenaline sensation. Admire the breathtaking scenery that spreads out along the beach while you sail the bay's turquoise waters with the wind in your hair.

Advice: Consider renting jet skis from respectable companies and abide by safety regulations.

9. Island-Hopping by Boat

Location: Several islands

Experience: Take an island-hopping trip to see Vanuatu's varied sceneries. Take a boat ride to nearby islands, each with its special beauty. The diversity of Vanuetu's archipelago is seen via island hopping, which offers access to isolated beaches, lush woods, and secret coves.

Advice: Arrange your island hopping schedule well in advance and think about taking a guided tour for a more tailored experience.

Dive into Aquatic Bliss

Adventure seekers and water lovers alike are drawn to Vanuetu's underwater treasures, which provide a world of breathtaking marine life and exhilarating activities. Every water activity and marine excursion, whether you're surfing at Pango Point, snorkeling in the Blue Lagoon, or going whale watching, reveals a different aspect of Vanuatu's enthralling waters. Put on your bathers, enjoy the sea wind, and let your underwater adventures in Vanuatu begin.

Cultural Events and Festivals

Numerous celebrations and events that honor customs, traditions, and a sense of community bring Vanuatu's cultural tapestry to life. This chapter delves into the vibrant schedule of cultural events that provide an insight into the essence of this captivating archipelago.

1. Vanuatu National Arts Festival

Location: Efate's Port Vila

Date: Annually in July.

Highlights:

- *Traditional Dancing Performances:* Take in mesmerizing shows that highlight Vanuatu's many dance traditions, complete with vibrant costumes and rhythmic moves.
- *Craft Exhibitions:* Visit craft exhibitions to see a variety of modern and traditional crafts, such as colorful woven linens and fine wood sculptures.
- *Music Showcases:* Lose yourself in the sweet tones of Vanuetuan music, which combines influences from the contemporary world with traditional instruments.

Experience: Artists, performers, and fans from all over the archipelago come together for the Vanuatu National Arts Festival, a cultural extravaganza. Participate in seminars, enjoy regional food, and take in the lively ambiance honoring Vanuatu's creative diversity.

2. John Frum Day Celebration

Location: Tanna Island

Date: 15 February

Highlights:

- *John Frum Procession:* Participate in the colorful parade honoring the legendary John Frum, which will include customary attire, dances, and ceremonies.
- *Gatherings for community feasts:* Savor the warmth and friendliness of Tanna's communities as they share traditional fare and regional delicacies.
- *Custom rituals:* Take part in customary rituals honoring the memory of John Frum, a significant character in Tanna's past and present.

Experience: Tanna Island's John Frum Day is a unique event that combines historical accounts with indigenous beliefs. Take part in the celebrations, make friends with the people, and learn about the cultural importance of John Frum.

3. **Naghol Land Diving Festival**

Location: Island of Pentecost

Date: April to June (precise dates vary)

Highlights:

- *Rituals associated with Land Diving:* Experience the breathtaking sight of land diving, when males from the area jump from towering wooden towers as part of a customary rite of passage while wearing vines wrapped around their ankles.
- *Cultural Performances:* Take in the ceremonies, music, and dances of the past that go along with the land diving customs for a complete cultural experience.
- *Community Get-Togethers:* Participate in shared meals and cultural interactions with the Pentecost Island communities throughout the festival.

Experience: The Naghol Land Diving Festival is a renowned occasion that highlights the courage and rich cultural legacy of the people living on Pentecost Island. Come to this exclusive event to see amazing land diving performances and get fully immersed in the customs of the surrounding areas.

4. Yam Festival in Ambrym

Location: Island of Ambrym

Date: Usually in June each year

Highlights:

- *Yam Harvest Celebrations:* As communities unite to celebrate the yam harvest, learn about the importance of yams in Vanuetuan tradition.
- *Custom Ceremonies:* Take part in age-old rites and ceremonies dedicated to the yam, a staple crop with significant spiritual and cultural value.
- *Cultural Exhibitions:* Take in displays of traditional crafts and artwork, such as finely carved wood and woven fabrics.

Experience: The Yam Festival in Ambrym is a feast for the senses that emphasizes the significance of yams in Vanuatuan spirituality and agriculture. Interact with the community, take part in celebrations, and learn about the cultural importance of this vital crop.

5. Independence Day Celebrations

Location: All around the country

Date: 30 July

Highlights:

- *Marching Bands and Parades:* Take in the vibrant parades honoring Vanuatu's independence that include marching bands, traditional clothing, and cultural exhibits.
- *Cultural Performances:* Enjoy dance and music performances that highlight the variety of Vanuatu's cultural heritage.
- *Fireworks and Festivities:* Enjoy the celebratory mood with street parties, fireworks, and get-togethers as we commemorate Vanuatu's independence anniversary.

Experience: Vanuatu's villages get together to celebrate Independence Day, a national holiday. Take part in the celebrations, indulge in the nationalistic zeal, and get fully engrossed in the pride and happiness that the islands have to offer.

6. **Maskelynes Canoe Festival**

Location: Islands of Maskelyne

Date: Usually in August each year

Highlights:

- *Canoe Races:* Watch traditional outrigger canoe races to see expert paddlers display their dexterity and camaraderie.
- *Cultural Displays:* Visit cultural displays that include elaborate masks, traditional dances, and storytelling that capture the distinct essence of the Maskelyne Islands.
- *Island Hospitality:* Participate in neighborhood gatherings, partake in customary feasts, and extend your gracious hospitality to the Maskelyne Island community.

Experience: The Maskelynes Canoe Festival honors cultural identity and marine customs. Take part in the celebrations, make friends with the people, and see how Maskelyne's cultural history is expressed in various ways.

Embracing Cultural Diversity

The celebrations and festivities of Vanuatu provide a glimpse into the diverse array of cultures, traditions, and narratives that characterize the archipelago. Every cultural festival, whether you're dancing to the beats of the National Arts Festival or seeing the fearless land dives during Naghol, urges you to absorb the essence of Vanuatu's colorful past.

Wildlife Encounters

Vanuatu's varied habitats, which include brilliant coral reefs, lush rainforests, and volcanic landscapes that weave a complex tapestry of biodiversity, provide a sanctuary for lovers of animals. This chapter takes us on an exploration of animal encounters as we learn more about the diverse species that live on this enchanted island.

1. Bird Watching in Mele Cascades

Location: Efate

Highlights:

- *Vanuatu Kingfisher:* With its characteristic blue and green plumage, the Vanuatu Kingfisher is a beautiful bird that is native to the islands. Look for its vivid colors.
- *Rainforest Aviary:* Take a tour of Mele Cascades' verdant rainforest surroundings, where a variety of bird species, such as fruit doves and lorikeets, contribute symphonies to the canopy.

Advice: For best sightings, carry binoculars, dress in subdued colors to fit in with the surroundings, and go birdwatching early in the morning.

2. Turtle Conservation at Tranquility Island

Location: Efate

Highlights:

- *Green and Hawksbill Turtles:* See the turtle sanctuary on Tranquility Island, where conservation efforts are concentrated on rehabilitating and safeguarding green and hawksbill turtles.

- *Guided Snorkeling:* During guided snorkeling sessions, explore the pristine seas around the island and come across turtles living in their natural environment.

Advice: Choose eco-friendly tour companies and keep a respectful distance from the turtles to promote responsible tourism.

3. Marine Life Exploration at Hideaway Island Marine Reserve

Location: Efate

Highlights:

- *Giant Clams:* Explore the Hideaway Island Marine Reserve by snorkeling or diving to see the magnificent underwater display of enormous clams' vivid hues.
- *Coral Gardens:* Discover the vibrant coral formations, seahorses, and reef fish among the diverse array of aquatic life that abounds in the coral gardens.

Advice: Wear sunscreen that won't harm the reef, go snorkeling responsibly, and think about taking a guided tour for an educational look at the marine creatures.

4. **Vanuatuan Flying Foxes in the Highlands**

Location: Several islands, including Tanna and Efate

Highlights:

- *Megabats:* The highland regions of Vanuatu are home to the unusual flying foxes, commonly referred to as megabats. These big fruit bats are essential for seed distribution and pollination.
- *Observing at Twilight:* As flying foxes take off for their nightly foraging trips, see the captivating spectacle of these nocturnal acrobats soaring to the sky.

Advice: In the highland areas, take part in guided wildlife excursions and observe the animals with awareness of their natural behavior.

5. **Volcano Safari on Tanna Island**

Location: Tanna Island

Highlights:

- *Volcanic Landscapes:* Explore the volcanic landscapes of Tanna and take in the hardy flora and animals that grow close to Mount Yasur, the active volcano.
- *Unique Insects:* Discover unusual bug species that have adapted to the volcanic environment, demonstrating the remarkable biodiversity of the area.

Advice: For deep insights into the local environment, think about taking a guided trip and heed safety instructions while venturing inside the volcano.

6. Reef Shark Encounters at Port Havannah

Location: Efate

Highlights:

- *Blacktip Reef Sharks:* Known for their elegant appearance in the warm, shallow waters, blacktip reef sharks may be seen while diving or snorkeling at Port Havannah.

- *Coral Reefs:* Discover the vivid coral reefs that serve as a home for a diverse range of marine life, including reef sharks and colorful fish.

Advice: Select knowledgeable dive operators while interacting with sharks, and conduct appropriate reef exploration.

7. Land and Sea Turtles in Espiritu Santo

Location: Santo Espiritu

Highlights:

- *Santo Turtle Sanctuary:* Come see conservation activities aimed at preserving both marine and terrestrial turtles at the Santo Turtle Sanctuary.
- *Release of Hatchlings:* Take part in or watch the release of hatchlings to help preserve these ancient animals.

Advice: Recognize seasonal turtle nesting and hatching phases and support local turtle conservation programs.

8. Ratua Private Island's Wildlife Reserve

Location: near Espiritu Santo on Ratua Private Island

Highlights:

- *Wildlife Sanctuary:* Discover the wildlife reserve on Ratua Private Island, which is home to a range of native and rescued species, such as exotic birds, iguanas, and coconut crabs.
- *Eco-friendly Practices:* Learn about the island's dedication to sustainability and conservation via eco-friendly programs that help the regional ecosystems.

Advice: Take part in island-based guided wildlife excursions and show appreciation for the work done to maintain and preserve Vanuatu's distinctive flora and fauna.

9. Dolphin Watching in Oyster Island

Location: Close to Espiritu Santo

Highlights:

- *Spinner Dolphins:* Watch spinner dolphins splashing about in the surf by going on dolphin-watching trips close to Oyster Island.
- *Opportunities for Snorkeling:* Dive with dolphins and explore the region's underwater treasures while snorkeling.

Advice: Pick trustworthy tour companies that provide appropriate dolphin interactions and follow regulations about interactions with animals.

Embracing Vanuatu's Natural Wonders

Encounters with Vanuatu's fauna provide a deep connection to the natural splendor of the archipelago. Experiences ranging from the vivid marine life to the unusual flying foxes and verdant rainforests provide a window into the complex ecosystems that make Vanuatu a wildlife enthusiast's paradise. So grab your snorkel and hiking boots, and let's go off on an amazing adventure across this magical place.

Day Trips and Island Hopping

The archipelagic appeal of Vanuatu entices exploration beyond the confines of each island, providing a wealth of opportunities for day trips and island hopping. This chapter takes us on a voyage of exploration as we learn about the variety and beauty that lie beyond Vanuatu's blue seas.

1. Iririki Island Retreat

Location: Efate's Port Vila

Highlights:

- *Luxurious Resort:* Reward yourself with a day of leisure at Iririki Island Resort, renowned for its breathtaking panoramic views and overwater cottages.
- *Activities on the Water:* Take advantage of the pristine seas around Iririki Island for kayaking, paddleboarding, and snorkeling.

Tips: To enjoy a day of luxury and peace, look into day ticket alternatives for using the resort's amenities.

2. Mele Cascades and Eton Beach Combo

Location: Efate

Highlights:

- *Mele Cascades:* Perfect for hikers and environment enthusiasts, Mele Cascades offers a verdant jungle and breathtaking waterfalls.
- *Eton Beach:* Unwind on the immaculate white beaches of Eton Beach, which has a gorgeous tropical environment with blue seas and swaying palms.

Advice: For the ideal balance of excitement and pleasure, combine the scenic splendor of Mele Cascades with a relaxed beach day at Eton.

3. Blue Lagoon and Moso Island Getaway

Location: Efate

Highlights:

- *Blue Lagoon:* Enter the pristine waters of this naturally occurring bathing hole surrounded by dense vegetation.
- *Moso Island:* Visit Moso Island for a peaceful getaway with serene beaches and a chance to get in touch with nature.

Tips: For a hassle-free day of exploring, sign up for a guided trip that visits Moso Island and Blue Lagoon.

4. **Port Olry and Champagne Beach Excursion**

Location: Santo Espiritu

Highlights:

- *Port Olry Beach:* This spot, known for its serene atmosphere and blue waves, is a great place to unwind.
- *Champagne Beach:* Visit Champagne Beach, one of the most stunning beaches on Earth, renowned for its pristine white sands and glistening blue seas.

Advice: Combining trips to Champagne Beach and Port Olry will allow you to spend a day fully enjoying Espiritu Santo's natural splendor.

5. **Hideaway Island and Coral Gardens Snorkeling**

Location: Efate

Highlights:

- *Hideaway Island:* Explore the underwater life and colorful coral gardens of the Hideaway Island underwater Reserve by diving or snorkeling there.
- *Glass-Bottom Boat Tours:* If you want to see the undersea treasures without getting wet, choose a glass-bottom boat trip.

Advice: Take advantage of both beginning and expert snorkelers' chances over a full day of exciting snorkeling excursions at Hideaway Island.

6. Pentecost Island Cultural Immersion

Location: Island of Pentecost

Highlights:

- *Naghol Land Diving:* Experience the breathtaking Naghol land diving ceremony, which is a customary rite of passage for the males in the area.
- *Cultural Experiences:* Engage with Pentecost Island people by taking part in cultural events and learning more about their way of life.

Advice: During a fully comprehensive cultural experience, schedule your visit during the land diving season, which runs from April to June.

7. Aore Island Adventure

Location: close to Espiritu Santo on Aore Island

Highlights:

- *Million Dollar Point:* Explore Million Dollar Point's underwater treasure trove, a World War II relic site including submerged military hardware.
- *Beachside Bliss:* Unwind on Aore Island's quiet beaches, which provide a tranquil getaway from the mainland.

Advice: Schedule a boat transport to Aore Island and see its historical and scenic attractions.

8. Tanna Island Volcano Safari

Location: Tanna Island

Highlights:

- *Mount Yasur:* Experience the unadulterated might of Mount Yasur, an active volcano known for its captivating lava displays and frequent eruptions.
- *Yakel Village:* Come interact with the locals and discover their customs by visiting Yakel Village.

Advice: For a secure and educational tour into the center of Tanna Island's volcanic landscapes, sign up for a guided volcano safari.

9. Ratua Private Island Day Pass

Location: near Espiritu Santo on Ratua Private Island

Highlights:

- *Wildlife Reserve:* Discover the nature sanctuary on Ratua Private Island, which is home to unique and rescued species.
- *Overwater Bungalows:* Bask in the quiet surroundings of Ratua and spend the day in luxury with access to overwater bungalows.

Advice: For a unique island experience, ask about day ticket alternatives to Ratua Private Island.

Navigating Island Delights

Day vacations and island hopping excursions in Vanuatu provide a wide range of activities, from thrilling volcanic eruptions to blissful coastal living. Every island adventure you take part in adds a new chapter to the fascinating tale of Vanuatu, whether you decide to explore the underwater delights of Hideaway Island or see the land diving ceremonies on Pentecost Island. So make your plans, head out, and let the island pleasures of Vanuatu entice you to explore and be amazed.

WELLNESS AND RELAXATION

Spas and Wellness Retreats

In the center of the South Pacific, Vanuatu invites visitors to go on a journey of well-being and leisure, where turquoise seas meet verdant scenery. This chapter introduces readers to the tranquil retreats, yoga ashrams, and seaside hideaways that allow guests to revitalize their bodies, minds, and spirits among Vanuatu's breathtaking scenery.

Spas and Wellness Retreats:

1. Lagoon Spa at Iririki Island Resort (Efate):

The Lagoon Spa at Iririki Island Resort is a peaceful haven tucked away on the coast of Efate. This spa, which is surrounded by the soft lap of the lagoon's waves, provides a variety of holistic services, such as restorative facials and massages. Savor the famous Vanuatu Taurumi Massage, which uses age-old methods to relax tense muscles and bring equilibrium back.

97

2. Champagne Ridge Wellness Retreat (Espiritu Santo):

The Champagne Ridge Wellness Retreat, nestled among the scenic hills of Espiritu Santo, offers a sanctuary for those in search of complete wellness. The tropical garden-surrounded resort provides yoga, meditation, and detoxification treatments as part of its health offerings. Relax while taking in expansive views of the Pacific Ocean's glittering waves and immersing yourself in customized wellness experiences.

3. Tanna Eco Wellness (Tanna Island):

Tanna Eco Wellness is a hidden gem on Tanna Island, where eco-friendly methods are practiced in balance with the environment. For treatments like massages and cleanses with volcanic ash, the spa here uses locally produced products. Participate in yoga and wellness seminars to establish a connection with the island's inherent energy.

Yoga and Meditation Centers:

1. Santo Yoga Shala (Espiritu Santo):

Yoga aficionados may find peace at Santo Yoga Shala, which has a view of Espiritu Santo's blue ocean. Yoga and meditation lessons take place in a lovely environment, captured by the island wind that flows through the open-air studio. To rebalance yourself, take part in guided meditation or yoga classes led by knowledgeable teachers in the morning.

2. Calm Spirit Yoga (Efate):

Nestled among lush tropical plants, Tranquil Vibes Yoga is a tranquil haven on Efate. Classes at this yoga studio vary from soothing yin sessions to energetic vinyasa flows. Take part in individualized plant-based diets, yoga, and meditation retreats for a comprehensive restorative experience.

3. Island Zen Yoga (Tanna Island):

Island Zen Yoga enjoys the tranquility of Tanna Island for mindful practices among its unspoiled settings. The yoga facility, surrounded by beautiful nature, provides daily lessons that combine conventional yoga with aspects derived from Vanuatu culture. In the middle of the forest, meditate and establish a connection with Tanna's primordial energy.

Beachfront Relaxation:

1. Paradise Cove Resort (Espiritu Santo):

Calm meets immaculate Espiritu Santo beaches at Paradise Cove Resort. Enjoy the peace of private beachfront homes, where the sound of the breaking waves acts as a soothing melody. With its beachside treatments and stunning views of the turquoise water, the resort's spa lets visitors relax to the sound of the waves.

2. Resort Breakas Beach (Efate):

The Breakas Beach Resort, located on Pango Beach's beautiful sands, is the definition of beachside tranquility. Savor yoga sessions on the beach while taking in the healing energy of the sea. Situated on the shore, the resort's spa offers treatments influenced by regional customs, guaranteeing a comprehensive approach to leisure.

3. Tanna Island's White Grass Ocean Resort & Spa:

White Grass Ocean Resort & Spa provides a retreat into the embrace of nature on the coast of Tanna

Island. Imagine yourself relaxing in bungalows on the beach, with expansive views of the Pacific Ocean all around you. Tanna's natural surroundings have the therapeutic potential to offer tourists, as its spa combines contemporary health with traditional techniques.

The Essence of Wellness in Vanuatu:

The health and relaxation options available in Vanuatu go well beyond opulent resorts and yoga retreats; they are woven throughout the islands. Rejuvenation-promoting factors include the calm trade breezes, the rhythmic sounds of the Pacific, and the dynamic vitality of the landscapes.

Vanuatu welcomes you to rediscover the art of relaxation, whether you choose to immerse yourself in the calming sounds of waves caressing the coast, find inner peace in a yoga shala by the beach, or find comfort in the embrace of a spa overlooking the lagoon. So give in to the island's charm, where health is a smooth fusion of age-old traditions and the treasures of nature, beckoning you to set off on a voyage of self-revelation and renewal in the heart of the South Pacific.

PRACTICAL TRAVEL TIPS

Health and Safety

In Vanuatu, where the allure of the islands is matched by a dedication to health and safety, visitors' well-being is of utmost importance. This chapter provides visitors with the necessary principles and considerations to put their health and safety first, enabling them to enjoy Vanuatu's delights with assurance.

Health Precautions::

1. Vaccinations:

It is essential to verify and update regular Vaccination records before visiting Vanuatu. Furthermore, it is advised to have certain Vaccinations, such as regular booster injections, typhoid, and Hepatitis A and B. To guarantee proper safety, speak with a medical expert well in advance of your trip.

2. Protection Against Mosquitoes:

It is important to defend against mosquito bites due to the tropical environment. Apply bug repellent, dress in long sleeves and slacks, and think about booking a place with screened doors and windows. Certain locations have malaria, so ask a healthcare professional about antimalarial drugs.

3. Safe Food and Water Practices:

Savor the gastronomic pleasures of Vanuatu while adhering to food and water safety regulations. To reduce your chance of contracting a foodborne disease, pick hot, well-cooked meals from reliable restaurants, stay away from raw or undercooked seafood, and drink bottled or filtered water.

4. Sun Safety:

Wear sunglasses, protective clothes, and sunscreen with a high SPF to enjoy the sun responsibly. To avoid sunburn and dehydration, drink plenty of water, particularly in the humid tropical environment, and find shade during the hottest parts of the day.

Healthcare Facilities:

1. Central Hospital of Port Vila (Efate):

The Port Vila Central Hospital offers both emergency medical treatment and general medical services in the capital city of Port Vila. The hospital's personnel may speak English well, and it is prepared to meet a variety of medical demands.

2. Hospital for the North (Espiritu Santo):

The Northern District Hospital is the main medical center in Espiritu Santo. It is best to have medical emergency and evacuation coverage with your travel insurance, as you may need to move to Port Vila for expert treatment.

3. Local Drugstores and Clinics:

Local pharmacies and clinics providing minimal medical supplies and services may exist on smaller islands. It is advised to seek treatment in Port Vila or Espiritu Santo for more serious medical issues, even if these facilities can be appropriate for mild illnesses.

Services for Emergencies:

1. Phone number for emergencies:

Dial 115 for an ambulance or 112 for general emergencies in case of an emergency. The operators on these phones may speak English and link you to emergency assistance.

2. Travelers' Insurance:

Having comprehensive travel insurance that covers medical emergencies, evacuation, and unforeseen situations is strongly recommended. Verify if the coverage for risky travel and aquatic sports is included in the insurance.

General Advice on Safety:

1. Safety of Water:

Be cautious while doing activities in the water. For water trips, choose reliable operators, abide by safety regulations, and wear the proper protective gear. Keep an eye out for marine life, currents, and local circumstances.

2. Traffic Safety:

When driving a rental car, abide by local traffic laws and drive on the left side of the road. When touring the islands, use caution—especially on gravel roads—and put safety first.

3. Sensitivity to Culture:

Honor regional traditions and customs. Ask for advice on proper conduct while visiting villages or taking part in cultural activities, in particular. A pleasant and courteous encounter is facilitated by modesty and cultural sensitivity.

Setting Out on a Secure Journey:

With an emphasis on health and safety, Vanuatu invites visitors to enjoy its treasures with its friendly hospitality and stunning surroundings. Travelers may have a voyage of exploration, well-being, and delight by emphasizing preventative measures, getting medical help when necessary, and adopting responsible travel habits. These travelers can go to the center of the South Pacific.

Packing Essentials

Packing sensibly is essential when traveling to Vanuatu to guarantee comfort, security, and the opportunity to fully enjoy your island experience. This chapter offers a thorough packing list that will help you make the most of Vanuatu's tropical weather, varied scenery, and unforgettable experiences.

Clothes:

1. Lightweight Garments:

Bring clothes that are breathable and light enough for the tropical weather. Fabrics like cotton and linen are great for staying cool, and long sleeves and slacks help shield you from the heat and bugs.

2. Swimsuits:

Pack an assortment of swimsuits for water sports, beach outings, and snorkeling. Fast-drying solutions are useful for traveling to other islands and touring.

3. Cozy Sneakers:

For beach excursions, choose water shoes, flip-flops, and cozy sandals. When organizing walks or treks, take into account wearing durable or lightweight footwear.

4. Rain Gear:

Prepare a poncho or lightweight, waterproof clothing for sudden downpours in the tropics. It may also be helpful to have a little umbrella.

5. Sun Protection:

Wear broad-brimmed hats, UV-blocking sunglasses, and high-SPF sunscreen to protect yourself from the intense tropical sun.

Safety and Health:

1. Travelers' Insurance:

Make sure your travel insurance is adequate and covers unforeseen occurrences, evacuation, and medical crises.

2. First Aid Package:

Stuff a basic first aid bag with important supplies including sticky bandages, antiseptic wipes, painkillers, and any prescription drugs that may be required.

3. Insect Repellent:

A trustworthy insect repellent containing DEET or other suggested components is crucial given the tropical environment.

4. Reusable Water Bottle:

Invest in a reusable water bottle to stay hydrated. Make sure the water is safe to drink, and for extra convenience, think about getting a bottle with a built-in filter.

Connectivity and Electronics:

1. Adapter:

To charge your electronics, bring a power adaptor that fits Vanuatu's electrical outlets.

2. Carrying Case:

Invest in a portable charger for your electronics, particularly if you want to visit isolated locations.

3. Water-Resistant Phone Cover:

Use a waterproof cover to shield your phone from sand and water, especially if you plan to partake in any aquatic activities.

Essentials for Travel:

1. Beach bag or daypack:

For outings, walks, and beach days, always have a daypack with you. Another helpful beach bag is lightweight and collapsible.

2. Empty Bags:

During aquatic activities, keep your valuables dry with waterproof dry bags for phones, cameras, and other necessities.

3. Travel Records:

Using a travel wallet, arrange and safeguard your passport, travel insurance information, airline tickets, and any necessary visas.

4. Money Transfers and Credit Cards:

Bring foreign credit/debit cards together with local currencies. It's wise to bring cash since certain locations can only take certain cards.

Equipment for Outdoor Adventure:

1. Equipment for Snorkeling:

If you're an avid snorkeler, think about packing your fins, mask, and snorkel for a custom fit.

2. GoPro or a waterproof camera:

Use a GoPro or waterproof camera to record moments of adventure and submersion.

3. Compact Towel:

Bring a small, lightweight towel for swimming and beach activities that dries quickly.

Items of a personal and cultural nature:

1. Items for Cultural Awareness:

Bring proper clothing while visiting villages or taking part in cultural activities to show respect for local traditions.

2. Toiletries in travel-sized containers:

Pack travel-sized personal hygiene products, such as toothbrushes, shampoo, and conditioner.

3. Essentials for a Daypack:

Stuff your daypack with necessities for day outings, such as a reusable water bottle, food, sunscreen, and bug repellent.

Other Items:

1. Pillow and blanket for travel:

Invest in a lightweight blanket and travel cushion to maximize comfort on lengthy flights or boat journeys.

2. Swiss Army Knife or Multitool:

From opening goods to engaging in outdoor sports, a multitool may come in helpful in a variety of scenarios.

3. Travel locks:

Use travel locks to keep your items safe, including your daypack and bags.

There's Adventure Ahead:

You can be ready for the experiences that lie ahead if you pack carefully and take into account the particulars of Vanuatu's activities and environment. Having the necessary items guarantees you may fully enjoy the beauty and sensations of this alluring South Pacific destination, from its sandy beaches to its lush jungles. So excitedly pack your luggage and get ready for an incredible vacation to Vanuatu!

Useful phrases for Travelers

Even though most people in Vanuatu speak English, learning a few words from the locals can improve your trip and help you build relationships with friendly people. This chapter includes some helpful words to get you through talks, show thanks, and fully experience Vanuatu's rich culture.

Basic Greetings:

Hello - "Halo"
Good morning - "Gud moning"
Good afternoon - "Gud afnun"

Good evening - "Gud evenin"
Good night - "Gud nait"

Polite Expressions:

Please - "Plis"
Thank you - "Tank yu"
You're welcome - "Yu welkam"
Excuse me / I'm sorry - "Sori"
Yes - "Yes"
No - "No"

Getting Around:

Where is...? - "Whea hemi...?"
How much is this? - "Hao maoch hemi dis?"
I would like... - "Mi laek..."
Can you help me? - "Yu save halp mi?"
I'm lost - "Mi gat los"

Food and Dining:

Menu - "Menyu"
Water - "Wota"
Food - "Fud"
Delicious - "Delis"
Bill, please - "Bil, plis"

Emergencies:

Help - "Halp"
Emergency - "Imajinasi"
I need a doctor - "Mi nid dokta"
Where is the hospital? - "Whea hospitol hemi?"

Numbers:

One - "Wan"
Two - "Tu"
Three - "Tri"
Four - "Fo"
Five - "Faiv"
The second is "Tu."

Expressions of Interest:

Tell me about your culture - "Plis, tel mi bout yu kalsa"
What is your name? - "Wat hemi nem blong yu?"
I love Vanuatu - "Mi lof Vanuatu"
Can you recommend...? - "Yu save rekomen...?"
Vanuatu is my favorite - "Mi lof Vanuatu"

Enjoying Nature:

Beautiful - "Biful"

Beach - "Bich"
Mountain - "Maonten"
Rainforest - "Renfores"
Sunset - "San set"

Expressions of Gratitude:

Thank you very much - "Tank yu tumas"
I appreciate it - "Mi presheeset"
You have a beautiful country - "Yudala gat wan biful kantri"

Navigating Activities:

Where is the beach? - "Whea bich hemi?"
I want to go snorkeling - "Mi wantem go snorkel"
What time is it? - "Wat taem hemi nao?"
Is it far? - "Hao long wea hemi?"
Can you recommend a good restaurant? - "Yu save rekomen wan gud restoran?"
Which regional cuisine is your favorite? - "Wat hemi falaet blong yu?"

Connecting with Locals:

What is your favorite local dish? - "Wat hemi falaet blong yu?"
I love your music - "Mi lofem miusik blong yu"

Can you teach me a few words? - "Yu save tisim mi liklik wod?"
Nice to meet you - "Nais blong mitim yu"
Goodbye - "Bai bai"

Embracing the Language:

Gaining some fluency in the native tongue may be quite beneficial for fostering relationships and demonstrating respect for Vanuatu culture. These words will enhance your trip and help you build deep relationships with the locals of this stunning archipelago, whether you're dining, seeing the scenery, or striking up a discussion.

Events and Celebrations

Vibrant festivals and festivities weave together Vanuatu's cultural tapestry, offering visitors a unique chance to fully immerse themselves in the way of life there. This chapter examines the wide range of activities that the Vanuatu islands host all year long, from contemporary festivals to customary rites.

1. Festival of Naghol Land Diving (Pentecost Island):

When: From April until June

What to do: Take in the breathtaking Naghol land diving ceremony, a centuries-old custom in which men from the area jump from wooden towers while wearing vines around their ankles. This distinctive cultural occasion is a sign of bravery and fortitude as well as a rite of passage.

2. Independence Day of Vanuatu (National):

When: 30 July

What to do: Join the nationwide celebration of Vanuatu's independence with parades, cultural shows, and customary rites. See the pride and happiness of the people as they unite to celebrate the history and uniqueness of their country.

3. Festival of My Roots (Tanna Island):

When: September

What to do: At the Back to My Roots Festival, take in the rich cultural legacy of Tanna Island. Take in the distinctive traditions and way of life of the island via traditional dances, music, and ceremonies.

4. Festival of Maskelynes Canoe (Malakula Island):

When: October

What to do: The Maskelynes Canoe Festival honors customary sailing and navigation and is held on Malekula Island. Savor colorful canoe races, cultural exhibitions, and the craftsmanship of locally built boats.

5. Port Vila, Efate - Port Vila Arts and Crafts Market:

When: Every Friday

What to do: Take a look at the handcrafted crafts of local artists at the Port Vila Arts & Crafts Market. This marketplace provides an insight into Vanuatu's creative past, showcasing anything from woven products to traditional wood sculptures.

6. Day of the Custom Chief (Various Islands):

When: Different islands have different dates throughout the year.

What to do: Learn about the importance of Custom Chief's Day, a ceremony that pays tribute to regional chiefs and their role in maintaining customs. Traditional dances, rites, and ceremonies are all part of the celebrations.

7. Agricultural Show of Vanuatu, Port Vila, Efate:

When: May

What to do: Visit the yearly Agricultural Show to discover Vanuatu's rich agricultural heritage. Discover the agricultural richness of the islands via farm exhibits, animal exhibitions, and cultural performances.

8. Festival of Gospel Music in Vanuatu (Various Islands):

When: November

What to do: At the Vanuatu Gospel Music Festival, experience a joyful and celebratory atmosphere. Gospel musicians from across the world come together for this event, which fills the air with spiritually uplifting music.

9. Market for Handmade Items by Women in Vanuatu (Port Vila, Efate):

When: Every Tuesday and Thursday

What to do: Visit the Women's Handicraft Market to see and buy amazing handcrafted goods produced by women from Vanuatu. This market provides evidence of the talent and originality of regional craftspeople.

10. Celebrations of Christmas and New Year's (National):

When: December

What to do: Take part in Vanuatu's Christmas and New Year's activities to experience the joyous season. Join the community's festive celebrations, which include customary meals, music, and holiday-themed activities.

Vanuatu's festivities and celebrations provide a dynamic tapestry of cultural diversity and community spirit, whether you're enthralled by the daring land divers of Pentecost Island or engrossed in the rhythmic rhythms of a gospel music festival.

To experience an extraordinary trip into the heart of South Pacific customs, schedule your visit around these celebrations.

CONCLUSION

When your journey through Vanuatu's captivating scenery and diverse cultural heritage draws to a conclusion, it's appropriate to pause and consider the experiences created among the azure seas, immaculate shores, and friendly locals. With its colorful customs and varied islands, Vanuatu has surely made a lasting impression on your travelog.

A Tapestry of Wonders:

The secret of Vanuatu's charm is its capacity to create a magical tapestry that enchants every tourist. Every island has a distinct appeal that is just waiting to be found, from the tranquil beaches of Tanna to the heart-pounding land dives on Pentecost Island. Vanuatu's remarkable destination is woven together by its rich cultural variety, which is more than just a feature of the island.

Cultural Immersion and Hospitality:

Throughout your trip, the warmth of Vanuatu's hospitality will never leave your side. Every tourist is greeted with an atmosphere of openness and community delight, whether they are participating in customary rites, enjoying local cuisine, or striking up a discussion with the always-smiling people. A profound respect for the customs that have endured throughout time is fostered and hearts are connected by the rich cultural heritage.

Outdoor Adventures and Natural Wonders:

Vanuatu's breathtaking natural scenery actively participates in your journey story rather than just serving as a background. Memorable experiences include trekking through beautiful jungles, snorkeling in crystal-clear lakes, and seeing the molten glow of an active volcano on Tanna Island. With its varied topography, each island beckons explorers to discover and experience the wild beauty that characterizes the South Pacific.

Culinary Delights and Market Treasures:

Traveling through Vanuatu is a culinary adventure for the senses. The gastronomic and cultural landscapes coexist together, from enjoying regional cuisine made with fresh ingredients to discovering lively marketplaces where craftspeople display their wares. The vibrant Arts and Crafts Market, the rich agricultural display at the Vanuatu Agricultural Show, and the Women's Handicraft Market in Port Vila serve as windows into the ingenuity and resilience of the islands.

Celebrations & Festivals:

Vanuatu's festivals and festivities are woven together into colorful tapestries that reveal the inner workings of the local communities. Every celebration serves as a window into the unique cultural essence of the islands, whether revelers are experiencing the traditional land diving process or dancing to the upbeat sounds of gospel music. These festive times enhance your trip and give you a better understanding of the resiliency and enthusiasm that characterize Vanuatu.

Peace and Well-Being:

Vanuatu's dedication to well-being and leisure is more than just a chapter—it's a recurring motif that fills the atmosphere. Travelers are invited to enjoy a holistic renewal via relaxing spa treatments, outdoor yoga sessions, and beachside getaways. The islands themselves turn into peaceful havens that provide a break from the bustle of daily life.

Conclusion

The experiences and the memories made become priceless mementos when you say goodbye to Vanuatu. This travel guide's sections are more than just instructions; they're stories that capture the essence of a place where culture and environment coexist together. Traveling through Vanuatu is more than just a physical experience; it's a cultural trip, an outdoor escapade, and a celebration of the little pleasures in life.

I hope the memories of Vanuatu will endure as a tribute to the beauty that results from the blending of cultures and landscapes. The colorful sections of this trip are just a peek at where the commonplace ends and the remarkable begins. You will always take the flavor of tropical fruits, the sound of laughing, and the beat of the island with you, and Vanuatu's embrace will always be a part of your journey.

Goodbye to Vanuatu, a paradise where stories of adventure are spoken by every wave, cultural legends are rustled by every palm leaf, and smiles emanate the warmth of a South Pacific welcome. May the recollections of Vanuatu remain a vibrant kaleidoscope of a trip well-traveled in your dreams till the next one calls.

Printed in Great Britain
by Amazon

42761628R00076